PRESIDENT MIRABEAU B.

LAMAR

Father of Texas Education

PRESIDENT MIRABEAU B.
LAMAR
Father of Texas Education

– Courtesy Austin History Center, Austin Public Library

By Elizabeth Dearing Morgan
Photographs by Nancy Dearing Johnson

EAKIN PRESS ★ Austin, Texas

To our publisher — ED EAKIN

our editors — MELISSA ROBERTS & MISSY DERKACZ

and our art director — TOM HAYES

for keeping Texas history alive

FIRST EDITION

Published in the United States of America
by Eakin Press
An Imprint of Sunbelt Media, Inc.
P.O. Drawer 90159 ★ Austin, TX 78709-0159

ISBN 0-89015-963-7

1 2 3 4 5 5 6 7 8 9

Library of Congress Cataloging-in-Publication Data

Morgan, Elizabeth Dearing.
President Mirabeau B. Lamar : father of Texas education / by Elizabeth Dearing Morgan : featuring photographs by Nancy Dearing Johnson.
p. cm.
Includes bibliographical references.
ISBN 0-89015-963-7 : $12.95
1. Lamar, Mirabeau Buonaparte, 1798–1859 — Juvenile literature. 2. Presidents — Texas — Biography — Juvenile literature. 3. Texas — Politics and government — To 1846 — Juvenile literature. [1. Lamar, Mirabeau Buonaparte, 1798–1859. 2. Presidents — Texas.] I. Title.
F390.L2M67 1994
976.4'04'092--dc20
[B]

94-2641
CIP
AC

Cover illustration by J. Kay Wilson

Contents

This is the statue of Mirabeau B. Lamar that overlooks Lamar University in Beaumont, Texas.

Foreword

Mirabeau B. Lamar, the father of Texas public school education, is a true Texas hero. He came to Texas as a pioneer before Texas became a state, he fought at the Battle of San Jacinto for Texas independence, and he served as a statesman and President of the Republic of Texas.

We are most proud of Mirabeau B. Lamar because he is the father of education in Texas. It was his leadership that created public school education in Texas. He believed that every child should be able to attend school and receive a quality education.

At Lamar University in Beaumont, Texas, we honor Mirabeau B. Lamar's name, his contributions to education, and his foresight in seeing that the children of Texas needed an education when this state was in its infancy. We proudly display a larger-than-life sculpture in the center of our campus for all to see. Engraved on the base of the statue are famous sayings from Lamar's lifetime.

We hope you will enjoy reading about a true Texas hero, and that, some day, you will visit our campus to learn more about this important man. Many of his papers are found in our library.

REX L. COTTLE, Ph.D.
President, Lamar University-Beaumont

This picture of Mirabeau B. Lamar was printed in the book of poems he wrote (see page 74).

— Copy courtesy University of Texas Institute of Texan Cultures, San Antonio, Texas

1

Growing Up in Georgia

Mirabeau B. Lamar was president of the Republic of Texas from 1838 to 1841. He was a hero at the Battle of San Jacinto and became known as the Father of Texas Education.

Mirabeau Buonaparte Lamar was born on August 16, 1798. His family lived on a plantation called Cherry Hill. It was near Louisville, Georgia.

His parents were first cousins. Their names were John and Rebecca Lamar. Mirabeau had an older brother named Lucius Quintus Cincinnatus Lamar. He also had two younger brothers named Thomas Randolph Lamar and Jefferson Jackson Lamar.

The four Lamar boys got their unusual names from their uncle Zachariah Lamar. He named them after whatever famous person in history he happened to be reading about at the time.

When Mirabeau later moved to Texas, the people there had a hard time trying to spell and say his first name.

"Fairfield," the Lamar family home, was built about 1808. Mirabeau last visited Fairfield in 1851. In 1890 the Lamars still lived there, and it remained a place of great beauty.

This photo was taken around 1936 by a descendant, Alexander Melrose Lamar (1887–1949). He rented the house to black tenant farmers, or share croppers. They lived in the house in exchange for giving him part of their crops. They chopped down the shade trees and planted cotton in the front yard of Fairfield.

In 1938, the house, "still unchanged," was owned by the Georgia Power Company. But they tore it down around 1960.

— Photo courtesy of Miss Nellie Lamar, Fort Valley, Georgia. Her father was Alexander Melrose Lamar.

He was named for the two greatest heroes of the French Revolution: Count Mirabeau and General Napoleon Buonaparte. But Mirabeau never spelled out his middle name. He just used the letter *B.* Because of this, some people said he was not proud to be named after Napoleon. This may have been true because long after Mirabeau was born and named, Napoleon made himself dictator of France and then tried to become emperor of Europe.

After the four boys, the Lamar family had five daughters. Their names were more plain: Louisa, Amelia, Mary Ann, Evalina, and Loretto Rebecca.

When Mirabeau was ten years old, his family moved to a new plantation. It was on the Little River, between the towns of Eatonton and Milledgeville in Georgia.

Their new house was called "Fairfield." It was a big, two-story house with a wide porch and white columns.

During the 1850s, people in Cahawba dropped the “w” and started spelling it “Cahaba.”

The Centennial Stone in Cahaba, Alabama, says, “Cahaba First State Capital 1818–1826. This stone marks the site of Cahaba, selected in 1818 as the first permanent capital of Alabama . . . remaining here until 1825.”

One hundred years later, in 1919, this stone was put up to celebrate the fact that, “As state capital . . . Cahaba was representative of the best in the life of a great commonwealth.”

— Photo by Nancy Dearing Johnson

Mirabeau went to school at academies in the nearby towns. He read a lot of history and literature. He also helped oversee the farm work on the plantation.

Horseback riding and fencing, or sword fighting, were some of Mirabeau's hobbies. He also liked to take boat trips up the Oconee River and stagecoach trips to Macon, Georgia.

As Mirabeau grew up, he acted in plays and went to dances. He wrote poems for many of his girlfriends.

In 1819, Mirabeau was a grown man. He and a friend moved to Cahawba, Alabama. They opened a store there. But Mirabeau's store soon had to close down, because it wasn't making any money. He then may have spent a semester teaching children at the Cahawba Academy.

Mirabeau also tried publishing a weekly newspaper. It was called the *Cahawba Press*. The newspaper didn't make any money, either. So he went back home to Georgia.

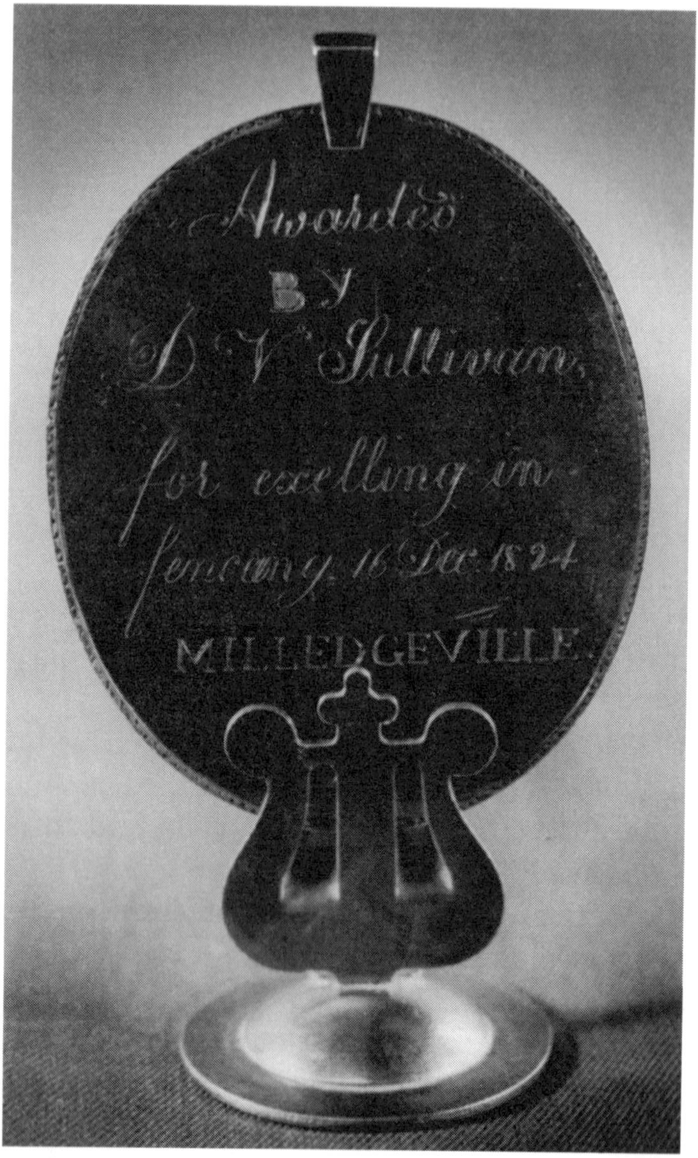

This is the silver medal Mirabeau won "for exelling in fenceing, 16 Dec. 1824 — Milledgeville." The engraver had fine penmanship, but poor spelling. It should read, "excelling in fencing." Mirabeau won this medal at age twenty-six in Milledgeville, Georgia. You can see it today at the San Jacinto Museum of History near Houston, Texas.

— Photo courtesy San Jacinto Museum of History, Houston, Texas

2

Mirabeau Marries

When he arrived back home in Georgia, an exciting election was taking place. It was to see who would be governor of the state of Georgia. George Troup won, and Mirabeau became Governor Troup's private secretary.

Governor Troup is best known for refusing to obey the president of the United States. They disagreed about how to handle the Creek Indians. Governor Troup believed that since the situation only had to do with Georgia, the president had no business getting involved.

During this time, Mirabeau organized a group of mounted riflemen (riflemen on horseback). He also won a medal for fencing.

Mirabeau and the militia got to be in charge of welcoming a famous person to Georgia. General Lafayette was a Frenchman who helped in the American Revolution. He visited America in 1825. Mirabeau was proud to meet the old war hero, so he wore a new sword by his side. Mirabeau had no idea that ten years later, he'd be a war hero himself.

The Crocheron Columns are all that is left of a magnificent home built around 1843. The columns were on the side porch of the house owned by the Crocheron family.

They are located in Cahaba, Alabama. Cahaba was deserted soon after the War Between the States. Now it is an archaeological park run by the Alabama Historical Commission.

— Photo by Nancy Dearing Johnson

Mirabeau had met a girl named Tabitha Jordan back in Cahawba. She was only fourteen years old then. He saw her again in 1824. He was surprised at how she had grown up.

Mirabeau asked Tabitha to marry him that same night, but she refused.

For over a year, Mirabeau kept proposing and finally Tabitha accepted. They were married on New Year's Day of 1826. Mirabeau was twenty-eight and Tabitha was seventeen. Tabitha's sister had the wedding at her home in Perry County, Alabama.

When Mirabeau and Tabitha were going back to Georgia, there was an accident. Something scared the horses and made them wreck the carriage into a tree. Tabitha was thrown onto some rocks.

Her face was cut very badly. Mirabeau took her to a nearby Indian hut. He got a needle and thread and gave her stitches.

The marker in front of the Columbus Ledger/the Columbus Enquirer building says, "The *Ledger-Enquirer* Newspapers. The *Columbus Enquirer* and the *Columbus Ledger* have been published from this site since 1930. The *Enquirer* was founded in 1828 by Mirabeau Buonaparte Lamar, later the second president of the Republic of Texas . . . Both have won the Pulitzer Prize for Public Service, journalism's highest award, the *Enquirer* in 1926 . . ."

The marker was put up in 1986 by the Historic Chattahoochee Commission of Alabama and Georgia and the R. W. Page Corporation, which owned both newspapers from 1930 to 1973.

— Photo by Elizabeth Dearing Morgan

George Troup's term as governor was over, so Mirabeau no longer had a job. He took care of Tabitha, and her face healed. It barely left a scar.

Tabitha had a baby girl on November 7, 1827. The baby was called Rebecca Ann Lamar, after her two grandmothers.

The next year Mirabeau and his family moved to Columbus, Georgia. He started a newspaper called the *Columbus Enquirer.*

He built a one-story wooden cottage. Mirabeau, Tabitha, and Rebecca Ann enjoyed walking along the Chattahoochee River.

In 1829 Mirabeau was elected state senator for Muscogee County. On August 1, 1830, Tabitha had a baby boy. They named him John Burwell Lamar, after his two grandfathers.

Mirabeau was going to run for senator again, but something terrible happened.

Tabitha's marker is in the Linnwood Cemetery in Columbus, Georgia. The front says, "Tabitha Jordan Lamar, wife of Mirabeau Lamar, daughter of Burwell & Anne Dupree Jordan."

The back says, "Erected by Mirabeau B. Lamar in memory of his wife whose death has left him no other happiness than the remembrance of her virtues."

— Photo by Nancy Dearing Johnson

3

Terrible Sadness

Tabitha died on August 20, 1830. She was only twenty-one years old. She suffered from tuberculosis, which affects the lungs.

Mirabeau was so upset that he withdrew from the race for senator, sold his newspaper, and closed up the cottage. He left Rebecca Ann with his mother at Fairfield, and John with Tabitha's mother in Alabama. He traveled around for two years.

Baby John passed away on July 31, 1831. He was almost a year old. He is buried in Perry County, Alabama. In 1832 Mirabeau came back to Columbus. He ran for Congress, but he lost. The next year he wanted to run again, so he did three things to help his chances.

First, he started the States Rights Party. This political party believed that a state had the right to decide whether an act of the national government was constitutional, or legal. They also believed that a state had the right to secede from, or leave, the Union.

On the left is the grave of Mirabeau's father, John Lamar. On the right is the grave of Mirabeau's sister, Evalina Lamar Harvey. They are buried near the site of Fairfield.

Mirabeau wrote the saying for his father's stone. Part of it says, "Here was a man of unblemished honor . . . a noble example of consistent virtue."

— Photo by Nancy Dearing Johnson

Second, he bought back the newspaper. That way voters could read about his ideas. And third, he got his license to be a lawyer.

The election had people arguing. Mirabeau saw one of his opponents shoot a political enemy on the streets of Columbus. Neither Mirabeau nor that opponent won the election.

Afterward, Mirabeau again sold the newspaper. That year his sister Evalina died. His father also died. But worst of all, his brother Lucius killed himself in 1834. Lucius suffered from depression. Mirabeau was so sad that for years after, he couldn't stand to hear the name "Lucius."

Feeling terribly gloomy, Mirabeau decided to go to the new land called Texas. He thought the adventure would lift his spirits.

Colonel James Walker Fannin was born in Georgia in 1804. He came to Texas to fight for her freedom. He and his men were killed after surrendering at Goliad.

This statue by Pompeo Coppini is in the Texas Hall of State at the fairgrounds in Dallas.

— Photo by Nancy Dearing Johnson

4

Incredible Bravery

Mirabeau came to Texas by stagecoach, riverboat, and horseback. He arrived in Nacogdoches on July 22, 1835.

He traveled all around Texas. The people were talking about getting their freedom from Mexico. He knew this was an important time in the history of Texas. So he started saving information. He collected letters, stories, and all kinds of official documents. This collection is called the *Lamar Papers.* It is now kept at the Texas State Archives in Austin. These papers are one of the most important ways people learn about the Republic of Texas.

Mirabeau agreed that Texas should free itself from Mexico, and he decided he wanted to live in this new land.

He returned to Georgia to make arrangements. There he received news about the fall of the Alamo. He also heard about the Texans who were murdered at Goliad. One of those Texans was Mirabeau's good friend, Colonel James W. Fannin.

The Twin Sisters cannons were a gift to the Texans from the people of Ohio. These replicas of the Twin Sisters were also a gift to Texas from an Ohioan and his wife many years later. The San Jacinto Monument looms in the background.

—Photo by Elizabeth Dearing Morgan

Mirabeau didn't finish his business. Instead, he hurried back to Texas. He got there in April 1836. He wanted to join the Texas Army. He rode his horse until it dropped dead beneath him. Then he set out, walking, to find the Texans. After a few days he caught up with the army. He joined as a private.

In a few more days, Mirabeau and the army reached a field, where they decided to camp. This field was soon to become the battleground of San Jacinto.

The Mexican army was camped nearby. On April 20, 1836, some of the Texans decided to try out their new cannons. Their cannons were named the "Twin Sisters."

The Texans and Mexicans began shooting back and forth. Some of the Texans decided to try to capture the Mexicans' cannon. Mirabeau and about sixty other men rode their horses across the field.

A lot of Mexican soldiers came out of the woods to protect their cannon. The Texans would have to go back without it.

This photo of Walter Lane was taken many years after the Battle of San Jacinto. He describes the event like this: "My horse — a powerful animal — had got excited, and, having more zeal that discretion, took the bit in his teeth and ran me headlong into the midst of the enemy, much to my disgust. The order was given to retreat. I was unanimously in favor of it, but my horse wanted to go through. A Mexican officer settled the difficulty by cutting at my head with his sabre. I threw up my gun and warded off the blow. My gun was empty. I drew a holster pistol, aimed at his head and pulled trigger. It missed fire; he tucked his head down to avoid the shot, when I hit him over the head with the pistol, knocking him senseless. Just then a big Mexican lancer charged me in the side, running me through the shoulder with his lance, observing: 'Carajo Americana' (d—n the Americans) and knocked me ten feet off my horse. I fell on my head, stunned and senseless. General Lamar rode up to succor me, shot the Mexican, and, thinking I was dead, fell back with the command."

— Courtesy Center for American Studies, University of Texas at Austin

But one Texan couldn't go back. A nineteen-year-old boy named Walter Lane had a problem. His horse did not want to retreat. It ran him into a Mexican officer.

The officer attempted to kill Walter with a sabre, or large sword. Walter threw up his empty gun to ward off the blow. Then he drew his other pistol and fired. But the bullet missed, so he used the gun to hit the officer over the head.

Just then a Mexican charged up and rammed Walter with a lance, or spear. It went in his shoulder, almost through the shoulder blade, and knocked Walter ten feet off his horse. He landed on his head and passed out.

Walter was on the ground. He had no way to defend himself. The Mexican rode over to kill him with the lance. Mirabeau dashed to his rescue. He saved Walter by shooting his attacker.

Mirabeau wounded his knee by hitting it against the pommel of a Mexican's saddle. But it wasn't too serious.

Carved into the San Jacinto Monument is a tribute not to Mirabeau the hero, but to Mirabeau the Father of Texas Education. He began the Texas public schools when he was president. "Lamar's School System" is shown in between the "San Jacinto Advance" and the "Building of Industries."

— Photo by Nancy Dearing Johnson

Thanks to Mirabeau, Walter lived and grew up to become a general in the Confederate Army. The Mexican lancer was seriously wounded.

Mirabeau saw another Texan in danger. Secretary of War Thomas J. Rusk was surrounded by Mexicans on horseback.

Mirabeau dug his spurs into his big stallion and raced over into the crowd. He knocked over one of the Mexican horses. This made a gap where he and Rusk could escape.

Mirabeau's actions were so daring that even his enemies cheered him. Being very polite, Mirabeau stopped his horse and bowed in front of the Mexicans. Then he and Rusk returned to the Texan camp.

That night the Texans were very excited. They talked about how brave Mirabeau was. But all they had to eat was dough rolled on sticks then baked by the fire and scraps from their pockets.

The San Jacinto Monument, built in 1936 to celebrate 100 years of Texas freedom, towers over the battlefield. Our three most recent national flags fly in front — the Lone Star of the Republic of Texas, the Stars and Bars of the Confederacy, and the Stars and Stripes of the United States of America. These words are carved into the stone: "On this field on April 21, 1836 the Army of Texas commanded by General Sam Houston, and accompanied by the Secretary of War, Thomas J. Rusk, attacked the larger invading army of Mexicans under General Santa Anna. The battle line from left to right was formed by Sidney Sherman's regiment, Edward Burleson's regiment, the artillery commanded by George W. Hockley, Henry Millard's infantry and the cavalry under Mirabeau B. Lamar. Sam Houston led the infantry charge."

— *Photo by Nancy Dearing Johnson*

5

The Battle of San Jacinto

The next morning, Mirabeau was promoted. He went from a private all the way to a full colonel in one day.

Mirabeau was in charge of sixty men in the cavalry. A cavalry is a group of soldiers on horseback.

The day was April 21, 1836. This day will never be forgotten in Texas history. It was the day of the Battle of San Jacinto.

The Texas commander was General Sam Houston. He had his army ready.

There were four men who made music. One was a drummer. The other three were fifers. The fife is like a flute.

They played a very popular love song. It was called "Come to the Bower." A bower is a shelter of leafy branches.

The words to the song are:

"Will you come to the bower I have shaded for you?
Our bed shall be roses all spangled with dew.

This painting of the Battle of San Jacinto, by Harry Arthur McArdle, hangs in the Senate Chamber at the Texas State Capitol. The artist interviewed Mirabeau's nephew to get a good idea of how Mirabeau looked at this battle.

— Copy courtesy University of Texas Institute of Texan Cultures San Antonio, Texas

There under the bower on roses you'll lie
With a blush on your cheek but a smile in your eye."

As the Texans marched into battle not only did they hear this song, but also they heard, "Remember the Alamo! Remember Goliad!"

The Texans swooped down on the Mexicans. The Mexicans were not prepared. Twenty minutes later, the battle was over. More than six hundred Mexicans were killed and two hundred wounded.

Only nine Texans were killed and thirty wounded. The Texan commander, General Sam Houston, was one of the wounded.

First, his big white horse "Saracen" was shot out from under him. General Houston got up on another horse and kept fighting. But this horse, too, was shot out from under him.

Then General Houston himself was shot. He was hit with a copper ball through the ankle. It broke two bones.

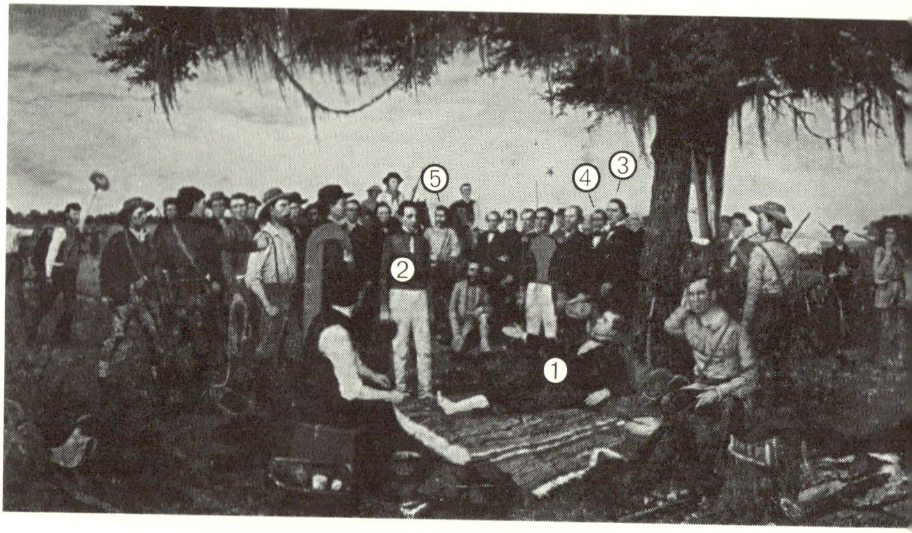

THE SURRENDER OF SANTA ANNA

General Sam Houston (1) lies on a blanket with his hurt leg. He accepts the surrender of Mexican dictator Santa Anna (2). Looking on is Secretary of War Thomas Jefferson Rusk (3), Colonel Mirabeau B. Lamar (4), and Lieutenant Walter Lane (5). This painting hangs in the State Capitol in Austin.

— *Copy courtesy of the University of Texas Institute of Texan Cultures, San Antonio, Texas*

The Mexican commander, General Santa Anna, was nowhere to be found. He was not only the commander. He was also Mexico's president and dictator, and the Texans hated him.

He had given the order to murder the Texans at Goliad. He also led the Mexicans when they took the Alamo.

After the Battle of San Jacinto was over, the Texans continued to round up Mexican prisoners. The next morning they brought in an ordinary-looking soldier.

"El Presidente!" the other Mexicans cried. The Texans had captured Santa Anna without even knowing it!

Now that they had Santa Anna, the Texans felt their victory was complete. But what would they do with him?

Mirabeau said that no matter how you look at it, "Santa Anna is still a murderer." But General Houston and Texas President David G. Burnet felt that Santa Anna was worth more alive than dead.

David Gouverneur Burnet (1788–1870) was president ad interim of the Republic of Texas. This means he was appointed president during the Revolution, to serve until an actual election could be held.
— Courtesy of the University of Texas Institute of Texan Cultures, San Antonio, Texas

6

Vice-President of Texas

Ten days after the battle, General Houston went to New Orleans to see a doctor for his ankle. The doctor took out twenty pieces of shattered bone. Thomas J. Rusk replaced Sam Houston as general. Mirabeau took Rusk's place as secretary of war.

The Texan government continued to argue about Santa Anna. Mirabeau wanted him executed, or killed, for murdering Texans. But General Houston and President Burnet thought they could use Santa Anna to keep the rest of Mexico's armies away from Texas.

Finally, Santa Anna signed a treaty. He promised never to fight against Texas again. He was allowed to go back to Mexico.

Two months after the Battle of San Jacinto, the president of Texas, David G. Burnet, promoted Mirabeau to the rank of major general in the army.

Because of Mirabeau's bravery, Secretary of War Thomas Jefferson Rusk lived to serve the Republic of Texas as major general and commander-in-chief of all Texas forces. He was also a lawyer, and after the Revolution, he was chief justice of the Republic of Texas Supreme Court. When Texas became a state, he served as her United States senator. This portrait hangs in the Senate Chamber of the Texas State Capitol in Austin.

— Copy courtesy University of Texas Institute of Texan Cultures, San Antonio, Texas

Mirabeau was supposed to take General Rusk's place as commander-in-chief of all the Texas forces. This didn't work out, and General Rusk stayed in command. But by the time two more months had passed, Mirabeau was elected vice-president of the Republic of Texas. Sam Houston was elected president. They took office on October 22, 1836, in Columbia, Texas. Mirabeau ended his speech on this day by saying, "Let our bright motto be God and our Country."

Mirabeau's headquarters were at Jane Long's boarding house in Brazoria. He and Sam Houston started having problems with each other after the Battle of San Jacinto. They didn't agree on what to do with Santa Anna.

While Mirabeau was Sam's vice-president, they had another disagreement. They didn't agree on whether the Cherokees had the right to be on northeast Texas lands.

This portrait of Mirabeau B. Lamar wearing his old-fashioned, baggy pants hangs in the Texas State Capitol in Austin.

— Copy courtesy State Preservation Board Capitol Collection Austin, Texas

Sam Houston had signed a treaty with the Indians before the war. It said they could have the lands if they promised not to help the Mexicans in battle. But the Texas government never approved the treaty, so Mirabeau didn't think it was legal.

The Cherokees had moved to Texas in 1821. They were not given title to the lands by Mexico, and after the war the Texas government had never given them title to the land, either.

So Sam and Mirabeau disagreed on whether the Cherokees could stay in the area that is now somewhere around Tyler, Texas.

Not only did Sam and Mirabeau have different opinions, they also came from different backgrounds. Sam was a western frontiersman, Mirabeau was a southern gentleman. For example, Sam usually wore buckskins. But Mirabeau was probably the only man in Texas at that time who wore the old-fashioned, very baggy pants.

•

This bronze statue of Mirabeau B. Lamar is in the Texas Hall of State on the fairgrounds in Dallas. It was created by Pompeo Coppini, the famous sculptor of Texas heroes.

— Photo by Nancy Dearing Johnson

7

The Campaign for President

Mirabeau's job as vice-president wasn't too busy. So he took a trip back home to Georgia. This was a year after the Battle of San Jacinto: April 1837.

When Mirabeau left Georgia, he was very sad because of all the deaths in his family, but he was coming back a proud hero.

The six months he spent in Georgia were filled with parties. The parties honored Mirabeau and the new country of Texas.

When he returned to Texas, his friends had an idea. They said he should run for president in 1838. Mirabeau agreed. Sam Houston could not run against him. Texas law would not allow the same person to be president two times in a row.

Sam Houston and his followers wanted a man named Peter Grayson to be president. But during the campaign, Grayson shot and killed himself with a pistol. He left a note saying that he suffered from depression. In those days they called it "melancholia."

On the back of this old photograph it says, "Site of Lamar home, Richmond. After the storm of 1900, rebuilt of material of original home on same site."

Today this home is just as lovely as it was in the last century. It is owned by the Hendee family at 915 Front Street in Richmond.

— Courtesy of The Center for American History,
The University of Texas at Austin

Then the Houston supporters chose a man named James Collinsworth. But he stayed drunk for an entire week and killed himself, too. He jumped off a steamer in Galveston Bay.

Just before the election, the Houston supporters chose a new candidate. His name was Robert Wilson. Mirabeau beat him with 7,000 votes to his 250 votes. David G. Burnet was elected as Mirabeau's vice-president.

Before Mirabeau took office, his daughter Rebecca Ann came to Texas for a visit. At the time she was eleven years old. She lived with Mirabeau's sister Amelia and her family in Georgia.

Rebecca Ann loved the shady yard at her dad's new home. He had just moved into the low, wood house on his plantation. He called it "The Oak Grove." He had a lot of visitors there.

One of his friends gave Rebecca Ann a pony. Mirabeau also had a little black galloping pony. He enjoyed it and rode it all over town.

This portrait of Mirabeau B. Lamar hangs in the Texas State Capitol in Austin.

— Copy courtesy State Preservation Board Capitol Collection, Austin, Texas

Rebecca Ann hated to leave Texas, but there were no schools for her to go to. So she went back to Georgia.

Mirabeau's Inauguration Day was December 10, 1838. This was the day he took over as president. It was Sam Houston's last day as president, so he made a speech.

The crowd expected Sam's farewell speech to be short. They wanted to hear what the new president had to say.

Sam showed up wearing knee-length pants and a powdered wig. He was dressed like George Washington.

Sam's speech told what he had done as president. It lasted for three hours. By the time he was through, the crowd was too tired to listen anymore.

Mirabeau knew it was no use to give his speech now. He had his secretary read it. He left and gave his speech before Congress a few days later.

This plaque at 405 Main at Preston in Houston marks the site of the first White House of the Republic of Texas. President Lamar lived there from December 1838 to October 1839. The state of Texas placed the marker in 1936.

—Photo by Nancy Dearing Johnson

8

Mirabeau B. Lamar

President of the Republic of Texas

The next month Mirabeau approved the official flag for Texas. The Lone Star flag was adopted on January 25, 1839. It is still used as the Texas state flag.

But not all of Mirabeau's work would be so fun. His job as president would be very difficult. Texas settlers were not safe from raids. The people on the frontier were attacked by Indians and Mexicans.

Some tribes, like the Shawnee, were paid to leave Texas. But the Cherokees wouldn't leave. The Texas Army had to fight a battle with them. Afterwards, what was left of the Cherokee tribe moved to Arkansas.

As soon as he became president, Mirabeau worked to create the Texas Navy. The Texans needed it to protect their coastline.

The Texan Flagship *Austin* was built in 1839. This sloop-of-war carried a crew of 300. The drawing was done by Midshipman Edward Johns of the Texas Navy.

— Courtesy University of Texas, Austin

Texas wanted Mexico to take it seriously. It would be too hard for the Texans to march thousands of miles across Mexican deserts to attack Mexico City. But the Texas Navy could easily attack Mexican sea ports.

Sam Houston didn't agree with this. He didn't think Texas needed a navy. He was just waiting for Texas to become a part of the United States. Then the Texans could use the U.S. Navy.

Nevertheless, Mirabeau got eight ships together, and the Texas Navy was at sea in 1840.

In one fight, two Texas sailing ships fought two Mexican steam ships. The Mexicans lost 150 men, but the Texans only lost five.

When Sam Houston became president again, he didn't want a navy. He said that the Texas Navy had fought without his permission. He called them pirates.

This enormous mural at the Hall of State in Dallas was painted in 1936. Mirabeau is pictured at the lower left. The painting symbolically shows that he is the Father of Texas Education.

— Photo by Nancy Dearing Johnson

The navy docked their ships in Galveston in 1843. The men had their names cleared in court, but the days of Mirabeau's Texas Navy were over. The ships were left to rot.

As president, Mirabeau made a statement about education: "Cultivated mind is the guardian genius of democracy."

This has become the most famous quote by a Texan. The University of Texas uses the quote as its motto. It means that to be free, people must be educated.

When Mirabeau became president, the government was in poor shape; it had no money. Texas Secretary of State Barnard Bee wrote, "Gen'l Lamar will have a trying time of it — Every thing is expected of him — and what can he do without a Dollar." But Mirabeau came up with a way to start public schools.

He had each county set aside some land. The money the land earned would pay for schools. The Texas Public School System was born in 1839. It is one of the best in the South.

Mirabeau founded the city of Austin by moving the capital there. The Capitol Building in the photo was built to replace the one that burned down about thirty years after Mirabeau died.

— Photo by Nancy Dearing Johnson

9

Moving the Capital

Another thing Mirabeau did as president was move the capital. It had already been moved to Houston, but he felt that was too far east. He thought the capital should be in the center of Texas. But where?

In the fall of 1838, Mirabeau had gone camping with some friends at a place called Waterloo. A huge herd of buffalo came near. Mirabeau chased the biggest one up the ravine and shot it with a pistol. The hunters gathered on the hill. They looked down at the wild rye grass and the Colorado River. Mirabeau said, "This should be the seat of Empire."

By 1839, Waterloo had a new name. The ravine was Congress Avenue. The spot where the hunters had gathered was Capitol Hill. Mirabeau founded the city of Austin.

There was a temporary Capitol, a President's Mansion, a business office for the president, and a Treasury Building.

This is what a Texas hundred dollar bill looked like. It is signed by "Mirabeau B. Lamar, Pres." in the lower right corner.

— *Courtesy Republic of Texas Currency 1838–1841 Antiqued Reproductions*

The Texans had to build a stockade around the Capitol. This fence or wall protected them from the Comanches.

Sam Houston thought it was a bad idea to put the capital in the wilderness. He wanted the capital to stay in the town that was named for him. But the city called Austin ended up being a good choice, because it was right in the center of Texas.

In 1841, Texas still had money problems. It cost a lot to protect the frontier from Mexicans and Indians. And it cost a lot to build the new Capitol and other buildings.

Many Texans were excited about a new project. They wanted to take a trip to Santa Fe to raise money. Today, Santa Fe is in the state of New Mexico in the United States, but back then it was owned by Mexico.

President Mirabeau B. Lamar is overshadowed in this mural at the State Archives by President Anson Jones. Similarly, Mirabeau B. Lamar is the only one of the three elected presidents of the Republic of Texas who does not have a statue outside the State Archives.
— Photo by Elizabeth Dearing Morgan

The Texans would trade with the people in Santa Fe. It would help bring money to Texas. The Texans would also ask if Santa Fe wanted to stop being ruled by Mexico. The Santa Fe area could become a part of Texas.

The journey was called the Santa Fe Expedition. Almost three hundred soldiers and merchants joined the expedition.

There were no good maps of the area back then. So the Texans thought Santa Fe was 450 miles away, but it was really twice that far.

The Texans ended up getting lost and running out of food. They had to eat lizards. Then they were captured by the Mexican army. Those who survived were marched to Mexico City and put in prison.

Because he was president, Mirabeau was blamed for the disaster. The newspaper published a letter saying that Mirabeau should be swapped to Mexico for the Santa Fe prisoners. It was signed only with the initial "A."

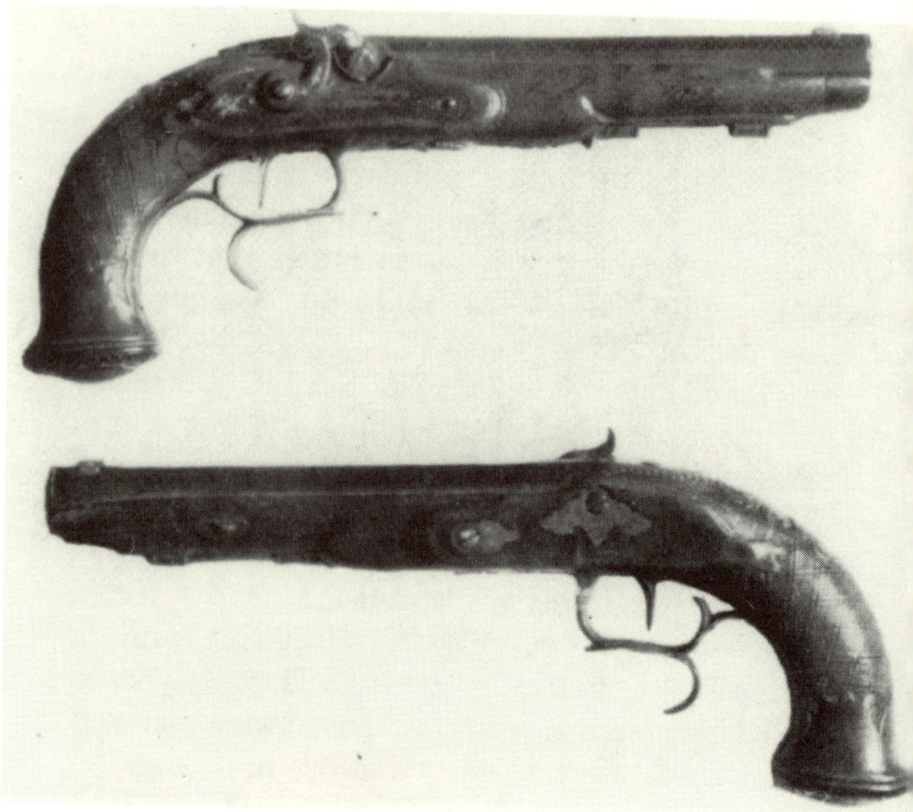

These are Mirabeau's dueling pistols. He may have planned to use them with Memucan Hunt. Today, the pistols are stored in the Texas State Archives in Austin.

This photo appeared in Herbert Gambrell's biography of Mirabeau.
— *Copy courtesy University of Texas Center for American History, Austin, Texas*

Mirabeau asked Texas Secretary of State Anson Jones if he had written it. Anson said that Memucan Hunt had written it. Memucan had been Mirabeau's Secretary of Navy.

Mirabeau challenged Memucan to a duel. But their friends helped work things out between them so they wouldn't fight.

There was another point that Mirabeau and Sam Houston disagreed on. Sam wanted Texas to join the United States, but Mirabeau believed that Texas could remain a country all its own, with no other rulers.

To stay an independent nation, Texas needed money. Money was so scarce that the Texas government couldn't pay the salaries of the legislators. They couldn't even pay the president.

It also needed other strong nations to agree that it indeed was a country all its own. When Mirabeau became president, only the United States recognized Texas as an independent nation.

The sign on the house says, "Legation de France." The historical marker says, "French Legation — Erected in the year 1841 by Conte Alphonse Dubois De Saligny, Charge D'Affaires for King Louis Philippe of France, to the Texas Republic. He lived here 1841–1842. House constructed of Bastrop pine, in Louisiana Bayou style. Furnishings included several pieces once owned by Saligny. Purchased by the State of Texas in 1945. Placed in custody of the Daughters of the Republic of Texas, who restored the house and maintain the property."

— Photo by Elizabeth Dearing Morgan

10

Crazy Happenings in Texas

While Mirabeau was president, four other countries recognized Texas. They were Belgium, the Netherlands, France, and Great Britain.

France sent a man named Alphonse de Saligny to represent the King of France. He built the French Legation in Austin. A legation is the official home or office of a diplomat.

France was going to loan Texas a lot of money. This would help Texas get a good, strong start as a nation.

But Alphonse didn't like Texans. He argued with the hotel keeper, Richard Bullock. They fought about a bill. Then some of Richard's pigs got into Alphonse's special corn and ate it. This corn was only supposed to be for Alphonse's fine horses.

Alphonse got mad. He told his servant to kill the pigs. The servant killed twenty of them. Then Richard got mad. He beat up the French servant. Alphonse had Richard arrested.

The plaque in front of the building says, "The Stable/Carriage House was reconstructed in 1974 as it was in the days of the Republic." The French Legation stable is now used as a gift shop by the Daughters of the Republic of Texas.

— Photo by Elizabeth Dearing Morgan

Richard was set free right away. So Alphonse moved away to Galveston. He felt it was more civilized there.

The "Pig Incident" seems silly now, but it was bad news for Texas back then. Alphonse was so upset that he told France not to lend the money to Texas, and they didn't.

Mirabeau had lots of challenges as president of a new country in the wilderness. But there were also fun times. While Mirabeau was president, the people of Austin played a joke on him.

He was usually absent-minded in the mornings. Mirabeau would walk from his house to the Capitol. One morning, groups of people called "good morning" to him. Everyone in the whole town seemed to make it a point to say "good morning" to him before he got to the Capitol that day. Just as he was about to go inside, one last group of young state employees surrounded him.

Anson Jones is most famous for being the last president of the Republic of Texas. This rare photo is owned by the Gonzales Historical Museum in Gonzales, Texas.

— Copy courtesy of the University of Texas Institute of Texan Cultures, *San Antonio, Texas*

"Good morning!" they all yelled at the same time. Mirabeau then realized that everyone was teasing him, so he took off his hat and gave a low bow. "Good morning, gentlemen; in the name of God, good morning to you all," he answered.

As Mirabeau's term in office ended, he was proud of the work he had done. He couldn't run for two terms as president in a row, so he went to live on his plantation in Richmond, Texas.

Anson Jones stated that Sam Houston wanted to make Mirabeau look bad. "He is willing the government should be a failure in order that he may have it to say there is no one but 'Old Sam' that the people can depend upon and that he is the only man that can successfully administer the Government of Texas."

Sam Houston was again elected president in 1841. He beat David G. Burnet. During the campaign, he called David a hog thief. For this, David challenged him to a duel.

This daguerrotype (an early type of photograph) of Mirabeau lets his clever personality shine through.

— *Copy courtesy of San Jacinto Museum of History, Houston, Texas*

Sam told David he'd have to get in line. Sam said there were at least two dozen men ahead of David who wanted to duel him. General Edward Burleson beat Memucan Hunt to become vice-president.

In 1843, Mirabeau went to Georgia. He visited his daughter, Rebecca Ann. She had missed him very much.

Soon after he returned to Texas, he was traveling on his horse. His friend and his friend's wife followed in a buggy. Mirabeau came up to a house. He told the lady he was an "old footman" and asked her for a cup of coffee. She told him no, and he left.

A few minutes later Mirabeau's friend caught up to this house. When he told the lady that she had turned away the ex-president, it left her "half-dead with mortification" or embarrassment.

Rebecca Ann Lamar is buried at Rose Hill Cemetery in Macon, Georgia. The front of her tomb begins, "Sacred to the memory of Rebecca Ann Lamar, daughter of Mirabeau B. & Tabitha Lamar, born Nov'r 7th 1827, died July 29th 1843. She was heaven's own. Her death translated her to the skies . . ."

The back says, "Adieu Dear Rebecca Ann, Earth mourns thee whilst heaven greets thee. Our hearts must ever sadden when we think of thee. Thou hast died so young, so lovely, so full of fairest promise."

— Photo by Nancy Dearing Johnson

11

"On the Death of My Daughter"

That summer, Mirabeau got a letter. His brother Thomas wrote: "Rebecca Ann has been taken from us — she is no longer of earth."

Rebecca Ann died on July 29, 1843, probably from yellow fever. Yellow fever was passed by mosquitoes, like malaria.

Rebecca Ann was only sixteen years old. Mirabeau was terribly upset. He wrote a poem called "On the Death of My Daughter." It told of how he looked forward to seeing Rebecca Ann again in heaven. Part of it says:

> "I long to pass the dull, cold grave,
> And wing my way to thee —"

The next year he traveled around the United States. He spent a lot of time writing poems.

Mirabeau spent the summer of 1845 in Macon, Georgia. There he asked Cassandra Flint to marry him.

This brooch, or pin, is part of a set of gold and jet "mourning jewelry." (Jet is a black stone.) This jewelry was worn by Mirabeau's wife when he died. The brooch shows a tiny picture of Mirabeau on the front. Inside, it contains a lock of his hair. You can see his hair at the back of the brooch. The jewelry is on display at the San Jacinto Museum of History near Houston, Texas.

— Photo by Nancy Dearing Johnson

His bride-to-be had heard some gossip. People said she wasn't good enough for Mirabeau because her parents weren't rich.

This hurt Cassandra's feelings. So she gave Mirabeau his ring back. It had nine diamonds in a cluster. Mirabeau wouldn't take the ring back. He wrote Cassandra a poem called "Gem of Delight."

Part of the poem says:

> "What gift shall I bring thee to merit thy love —
> Some pearl from the ocean, or star from above?"

Mirabeau ended up returning to Texas alone. By this time, Texas had joined the United States, which caused the Mexican War. Mexico felt like the United States was taking its land. The United States felt that Texas was free as an independent republic and didn't belong to Mexico anymore.

Mirabeau signed up to fight under General Zachary Taylor. General Taylor later became a United States president.

From a daguerreotype

Mirabeau B. Lamar in 1845

COURTESY OF MR. LUCIUS Q. C. LAMAR, HAVANA

This photo is from a book called *The Life and Poems of Mirabeau B. Lamar.* It was written by Philip Graham in 1938.

— Photo reproduced courtesy of James Marshall, Jr., President, Eatonton-Putnam County Historical Society, Inc.

12

The Mexican War

Mirabeau was an inspector-general. He led a charge at the Battle of Monterey. He rallied the Americans in front of the bishop's palace. Jefferson Davis said he expected every instant to see Mirabeau riddled with bullets. The gold and red vest Mirabeau wore at Monterey became famous.

Later in the war, Mirabeau organized a group of men at Laredo. They were to protect the frontier.

When one of these soldiers started up a hill to see if they were going to be ambushed, Mirabeau stopped him. "Don't you know that they will kill you up there! Let me go," he told the soldier. And then Mirabeau himself went.

Mirabeau was not satisfied with staying on the border. He and his soldiers wanted to go into Mexico. They felt fighting in Mexico was more important than guarding the frontier. Mirabeau blamed Sam Houston, who was now a United States senator, for holding him back.

This is a picture of Mirabeau's second wife, Henrietta Maffitt Lamar. She lived from 1827 to 1891.

— Photo courtesy Daughters of the Republic of Texas Library, DeShields Collection, San Antonio, Texas

Sam Houston could suggest assignments to the United States president, but he and Mirabeau still didn't get along. Sam had long ago been given the nickname "Big Drunk."

Mirabeau was unhappy to have to stay in Laredo. This caused him to write, "I can regard Texas as very little more than Big Drunk's big Ranch."

During his last year in Laredo, Mirabeau also served as a representative from Nueces and San Patricio counties. Then he retired to his plantation in Richmond, Texas. He also traveled. In 1851 he was staying with friends in New Orleans. Another guest staying in the house was Miss Henrietta Maffitt of Galveston. Her father, John Maffitt, was a very famous preacher.

Henrietta was engaged to marry a man in Galveston. But Mirabeau wrote her some love poems. In a few weeks, she agreed to marry him instead. He was fifty-three years old, and she was twenty-four.

This is a photo of Loretto Evalina Lamar after she had grown up and become a grandmother. It is from a 1936 article in the *San Antonio Express* called "To the Ladies of the House of Lamar." The caption said, "Lamar's daughter and great-granddaughter, Mrs. Loretto Lamar Calder and Katherine Calder." Loretto's grandbaby was born long after Mirabeau had died.

— *Photo courtesy* San Antonio Express-News

13

United States Minister to Nicaragua

Mirabeau and Henrietta took a wedding trip to Columbus, Milledgeville, and Fairfield (all in Georgia).

But they spent most of 1851 in Macon, Georgia. This is where Mirabeau's first daughter, Rebecca Ann, lay buried. And here, in 1852, a second daughter was born. They named her Loretto Evalina, after two of Mirabeau's sisters.

They moved to Mirabeau's plantation in Richmond, Texas. They had money problems. Henrietta earned a little money by selling butter. She made the butter from cream produced by their cows. Though times were tough, Mirabeau's family was very happy.

Late in 1852, United States President Pierce needed a secretary of war. He had to choose between Mirabeau and Colonel Jefferson Davis. He ended up choosing Jefferson.

But Mirabeau got to serve the United States later. In 1857, U.S. President Buchanan offered Mirabeau a job as a diplomat. He would be United States minister to Nicaragua and Costa Rica.

The author is holding a copy of Mirabeau B. Lamar's book of poems, *Verse Memorials.* Mirabeau had it published in New York City in 1857. Across from the title page are his picture and signature.

This book is in the Columbus College Library in Columbus, Georgia.
— *Photo by Nancy Dearing Johnson*

The job would pay enough to support his family. Although Mirabeau would miss Henrietta and Loretto, he took the job.

Before he left, in 1857, he had his many poems published into a book. He called it *Verse Memorials.*

Early in 1858 he was in Managua, Nicaragua, with his family far away. The next year he was criticized in a northern newspaper. It said he was "openly lying in a public warehouse without hat, coat, shoes, or stockings."

He had become a part of the frontier by living in Texas. He had gotten used to taking his afternoon nap on his front porch. He would stretch out on the wood floor with his hat as his pillow. So the newspaper may have been correct, or it may have just been saying things about him because he was a southerner.

This statue of Lamar is on the Fort Bend County Courthouse lawn in Richmond, Texas. It was put up in 1936 to celebrate one hundred years of Texan independence from Mexico.

On the back, it says, "Mirabeau Buonaparte Lamar — the Father of Education in Texas — Born in Georgia August 16, 1798 — Founded the *Columbus Enquirer* — Came to Texas in 1836 — He commanded the cavalry at the Battle of San Jacinto — Served successively as Secretary of War — Vice President and President of the Republic of Texas — Secured a public endowment for schools — academies and a university — Fought with distinction in the Mexican War — Served in the Texas Legislature and as minister to Nicaragua — Died in Richmond, Texas on the 19th day of December 1859."

— Photo by Elizabeth Dearing Morgan

14

At Home in Richmond

Almost two years later, Mirabeau got sick and quit his job as a diplomat. He returned to the plantation in October 1859. He brought Loretto a monkey and a parrot. The parrot was very loyal to Loretto. It would attack her uncle, Dr. Alexander, because it didn't like him much.

The Lamars were happy again. They were getting ready for the Christmas season when Mirabeau became ill.

A doctor was called, and Mirabeau told him, "I feel very queerly; I believe I am going to die."

At ten o'clock that day, December 19, 1859, President Mirabeau B. Lamar was dead. He had a heart attack at age sixty-one.

The loss to Texas was sure. Mirabeau was one of its founding patriots — the president who was a hero at the Battle of San Jacinto and the Father of Texas Education.

The historical marker for Morton Cemetery says, "Burial place of illustrious pioneers, including 1838–1841 Republic of Texas President Mirabeau B. Lamar (1798–1859) . . ."

Mirabeau's tall marker is on the left. On the back it has a shield that says, "Lamar." On the front it says, "Ex-President of Texas. Died Dec. 19, 1859: Aged 61 Years, 4 Mo's & 2 days." The marker was blown down in the great storm of 1900 and not put back up until after 1904.

The grave with the cross is where his wife is buried. On the back it says, "I.H.S." for "In His Service." On the front it says, "Henrietta Lamar, wife of M. B. Lamar, Ex-President of Texas. Died Oct. 8, 1891."

Their daughter Loretto is buried just in front of them. Her marker says, "Loretto Lamar Calder, 1853–1933."

About twenty years ago, a couple of people reported hearing mysterious organ music while standing at Lamar's grave.

It could have been from the other side of the grave, or from the other side of the tracks.

— Photo by Elizabeth Dearing Morgan

The loss to the South can only be imagined. Two years after Mirabeau's death, eleven southern states joined together to become the Confederate States of America.

This Confederacy included Mirabeau's home states of Georgia, Alabama, and Texas. The Confederate States fought for their states' rights against the northern United States. This struggle was called the War Between the States, and it lasted from 1861 to 1865.

Jefferson Davis became president of the Confederate States of America. Jefferson and Mirabeau were both Mexican War heroes. If Mirabeau had lived, he may have been president of the Confederacy instead. This would have allowed Jefferson to be a general on the battlefield, as he had wished.

Mirabeau is buried in Richmond, Texas. No one can know how he might have helped the South. But he will always be remembered as the southern gentleman who shaped the great Republic of Texas.

Lamar Schools

Mirabeau B. Lamar has almost forty schools named for him in Texas. Many school districts have a policy of naming schools for Texas heroes. Mirabeau, as the second elected president of Texas, qualifies in that regard. But he is also remembered because, as the Father of Texas Education, it was he who started the entire free education system in the state. Many Texans today have attended schools named for Lamar, who is honored for his concern for Texas school children.

The first school to be named for Mirabeau was Lamar Elementary School in El Paso I.S.D. It was opened in 1906. A new building on a new site was built in 1962. The old building was torn down, but five stained glass windows from the old building were saved and used in the new building.

Lamar Elementary School in Greenville I.S.D. was built in 1922. They had a seventieth birthday celebration in 1992.

Two schools were named for Mirabeau in 1924. Mirabeau Lamar Elementary was opened in San Antonio I.S.D., but was closed in 1975 because there were not enough students in the Mahncke Park neighborhood. Happily, it reopened in 1985 when more children moved to the downtown area.

Lamar Primary School in New Braunfels I.S.D.

was the other school built in 1924, with an addition built in 1951.

Goose Creek I.S.D.'s Lamar Elementary in Baytown was built in 1930.

East Ward, built in 1913, is the oldest elementary school in Kingsville I.S.D. In 1931, it was renamed: Mirabeau B. Lamar Elementary.

Houston I.S.D.'s Lamar High School opened in 1937, and Houston's Lamar Elementary School was built in 1962. Additionally, Houston I.S.D.'s Woodrow Wilson Elementary School stands on the site of President Lamar's summer home (2100 Yupon).

Bryan I.S.D.'s Lamar Junior High was built in 1938. It moved to a new building in 1957. It is now the Lamar Ninth Grade Campus of Bryan High School.

Ector County I.S.D. has a Lamar campus that was built in 1940. It now serves more than 500 prekindergartners as the Lamar Early Education Center in Odessa.

Corpus Christi I.S.D.'s Lamar Elementary opened in 1941.

In 1944, McAllen High School was converted and renamed for Mirabeau. Today it is Lamar Middle School.

In 1947, an entire school district was named for Mirabeau. It is Lamar Consolidated I.S.D. in Fort Bend County. Lamar Consolidated High School (built in 1949) and Lamar Junior High (built in 1959) serve the sister cities of Richmond and Rosenberg.

Sulphur Springs I.S.D.'s North Elementary School was renamed Lamar Elementary School in 1948. In 1967 a new building was constructed.

Also opened in 1948 was Denton I.S.D.'s Lamar Elementary.

In 1949, Lamar Intermediate opened in San Marcos C.I.S.D.

During the 1950s, Mirabeau was honored with quite a few schools:

Amarillo I.S.D., Mirabeau B. Lamar Elementary School, 1951 (renovated 1988)
Midland I.S.D., Lamar Elementary, 1951
Grand Prairie I.S.D., Lamar Elementary School, 1952
Pecos-Barstow-Toyah I.S.D., Lamar Elementary, 1953
Mineral Wells I.S.D., Lamar Elementary, 1954
Pampa I.S.D., Lamar Elementary, 1954
Austin I.S.D., Lamar Middle School, 1955
Harlingen C.I.S.D., Lamar Elementary, 1955 (renovated 1961, 1968, 1972, 1988, and 1993)
Temple I.S.D., Lamar Middle School, 1956
Edinburg C.I.S.D., Lamar Elementary School, 1956
Sinton I.S.D., Lamar Elementary School, 1956
Laredo I.S.D., Lamar Middle School, 1957
Port Arthur I.S.D., Lamar Elementary, 1957, changed to Lamar Community Guidance Center in 1973
San Felipe-Del Rio C.I.S.D., Lamar Elementary, 1958
Wichita Falls I.S.D., Lamar Elementary, 1958

In 1970, Mirabeau was honored with another school and district: North Lamar High School and North Lamar I.S.D. in Paris, Lamar County, Texas.

Also opening in 1970 was Arlington I.S.D.'s Lamar High School.

In 1971, two more schools were added: Mirabeau Lamar Junior High in Irving I.S.D. and Conroe I.S.D.'s Lamar Elementary School in The Woodlands.

The most recent naming of a school for the Father of Texas Education was in 1987: Lamar Middle School in Lewisville I.S.D.

Mirabeau even has a college named for him. Lamar University in Beaumont first opened in 1923 as a junior college and became a senior college in 1951.

The "Mirabeau Buonaparte Lamar — President of the Republic of Texas" marker stands in front of Lamar Consolidated High School (Lamar C.I.S.D.) in Rosenberg, Texas.

— Photo by Elizabeth Dearing Morgan

Lamar Day

The Daughters of the Republic of Texas (DRT) are women whose ancestors were loyal Texas citizens before Texas became a state in 1846. Their goal is to promote the memory of Texas pioneer families and soldiers of the Republic of Texas.

They celebrate Texas Honor Days throughout the year. One of these days is in honor of Mirabeau. January 26th was chosen as Lamar Day to celebrate the date in 1839 when Mirabeau signed the Texas public schools into being.

This is the Lamar–Calder Cottage in Richmond, Texas, today. Compare it to the old photo on page 38.

— Photo by Elizabeth Dearing Morgan

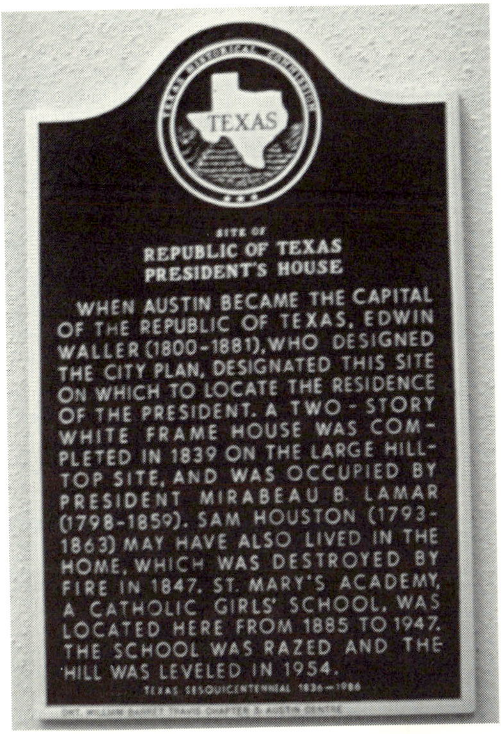

This marker, "Site of Republic of Texas President's House," is inside the Omni Hotel at 700 San Jacinto in downtown Austin. It says, ". . . A two-story white frame house was completed in 1839 on the large hilltop site, and was occupied by President Mirabeau B. Lamar (1798–1859) . . . The home was destroyed by fire in 1847 . . . The hill was leveled in 1954."

— Photo by Nancy Dearing Johnson

The marker for "All Saints' Episcopal Church" says, "The edifice stands on the mid-1840s land grant of Texas President Mirabeau B. Lamar . . . All Saints' Chapel was built in 1899." The Gothic church is located at 27th and Whitis in the University of Texas area of Austin.

— Photo by Nancy Dearing

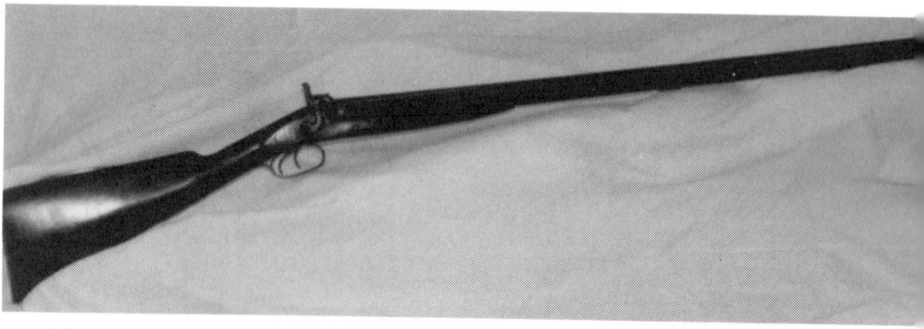

This is Mirabeau's 10-gauge double-barreled shotgun that he ordered from England in 1828. He probably used it at the Battle of San Jacinto. If so, it was the largest piece of artillery there except for the Twin Sisters. The nameplate on the three and one-half foot long gun misspells his name "Maribeau B. Lamar 1828." The gun is stored at the Texas Memorial Museum, University of Texas at Austin.

— *Photo by Nancy Dearing Johnson*

This stone marks the site of Mirabeau's home in Richmond from 1851 to his death in 1859. It is next to the Lamar–Calder cottage, which he began building before he died.

— *Photo by Elizabeth Dearing Morgan*

Lamar County

In 1840, Mirabeau had a county named after him. It was 894 square miles of land that was taken from huge Red River County. The land is between the Red and Sulphur rivers. In the middle of Lamar County is its county seat: Paris, Texas.

Mirabeau also has a town named for him: Lamar, Texas, in Refugio County. Lamar, Texas, rests on a peninsula between Copano Bay and Aransas Bay.

Another Famous Lamar

Mirabeau is not the only Lamar to have a county named for him. Lamar County, Georgia, and Lamar County, Mississippi, are named for his nephew, Lucius Quintus Cincinnatus, Jr., who was born at Fairfield in 1825. Lucius, Jr., was a United States senator and United States Supreme Court justice before his death in 1893.

The Georgia Historical Commission put up this marker for Mirabeau Buonaparte Lamar in Columbus, Georgia, 1953.

— *Photo courtesy Billy Winn,* Columbus Ledger–Enquirer

Books by or About Mirabeau B. Lamar

Christian, Asa Kyrus. *Mirabeau Buonaparte Lamar.* Austin: Von Boeckmann-Jones, 1922.

Gambrell, Herbert Pickens. *Mirabeau Buonaparte Lamar: Troubador & Crusader.* Dallas: Southwest Press, 1934.

Graham, Philip. *The Life and Poems of Mirabeau B. Lamar.* Chapel Hill: The University of North Carolina Press, 1938.

Gulick, Charles Adams, Jr. et al, editor. *Papers of Mirabeau Buonaparte Lamar,* 6 volumes. Austin: Pemberton Press, 1968.

Lamar, Mirabeau Buonaparte. *Verse Memorials.* New York: W. P. Fetridge and Company, 1857.

Ramsay, Jack C., Jr. *Thunder Beyond the Brazos: Mirabeau B. Lamar, a Biography.* Austin: Eakin Press, 1985.

Siegel, Stanley. *The Poet President of Texas.* Austin: Pemberton Press, 1977.

West, Elizabeth Howard. *The Calendar of the Papers of Mirabeau Buonaparte Lamar.* Austin: Von Boeckmann-Jones, 1914.

Glossary

academy — a place for learning
archaeological park — park where you can study the people, customs, and life of old times
archives — place where public records or historical documents are kept
buckskin — clothing made of deer or sheep leather
column — pillar or post
commonwealth — a state
consistent virtue — habitual goodness
discretion — good judgment
frontiersman — man who lives on the last edge of settled country
plantation — large farm
pommel — part of a saddle that sticks up at the front
republic — nation
revolution — complete overthrow of an established government
semester — half of a school year
succor — help
treaty — agreement
unblemished honor — spotless honesty
zeal — enthusiasm

Acknowledgments

Thank you to those members of our family who endured out-of-town research trips with us: our husbands, Tom Morgan and Louis Johnson; our sons, Clint Morgan and Justin Johnson; our brother and his family, Clyde, Tamra, and Travis Dearing; and our parents, Jo Anne and Olin Dearing.

Thank you to Linda Derry, park manager and archaeologist at Old Cahawba Archaeological Park near Selma, Alabama.

Thank you to Becky Bassett of the Georgia Department of Tourism, and to the Columbus Convention and Visitors Bureau. Also, thank you to Columbus College Library and Holiday Inn Airport in Columbus, Georgia.

Thank you to Becky Morris of the Georgia Department of Tourism, and to the Macon Convention and Visitors Bureau. Also, thank you to Comfort Inn North and to Larry Fortson for his help at Rose Hill Cemetery in Macon, Georgia.

Thank you to James Marshall, Jr., president of the Eatonton-Putnam County Historical Society and to Emory Lavender, publisher of *The Countryman* newspaper, for taking us to the site of Fairfield in Eatonton, Georgia.

Also thanks to Tom Shelton of the U.T. Institute of Texan Cultures for his help with photographs.

Index

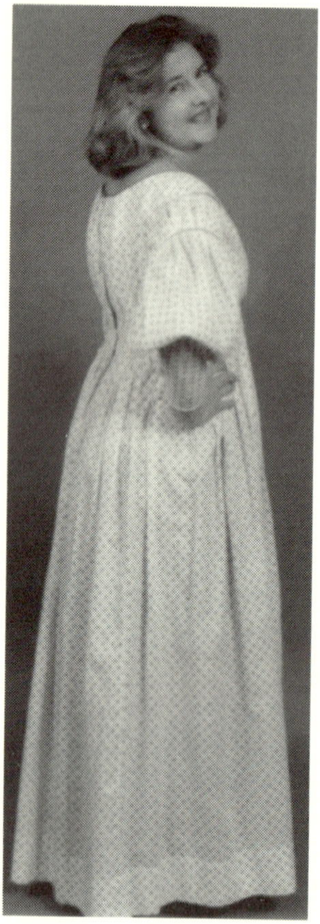

ELIZABETH DEARING MORGAN

ABOUT THE AUTHOR

Elizabeth Dearing Morgan and her sister, Nancy Dearing Johnson, have traveled throughout Texas, Alabama, and Georgia researching the life of Mirabeau B. Lamar.

Their previous book in this series is *Jane Long: A Child's Pictorial History*. It is a photobiography of the Mother of Texas, who was Mirabeau B. Lamar's close friend.

Elizabeth Morgan is a Texas secondary schoolteacher, certified in social studies, reading, English, business, and home economics. She teaches at the Del Valle Opportunity Center, which, when built in 1957, served as Lamar Elementary School.

She is a member of the Daughters of the Republic of Texas, the United Daughters of the Confederacy, and the Daughters of the American Revolution. She lives in Austin.

Morgan and Johnson offer various programs for children and adults. For author visits or study guides, call the publisher at 512 / 288-1771.

— Photo by John Neely